T0199144

Memoirs of the Soul Searcher

Anna Elena Gordon

WESTBOW
PRESS®
A DIVISION OF THOMAS NELSON
& ZONDERVAN

WestBow Press books may be ordered through booksellers or by contacting:

WestBow Press
A Division of Thomas Nelson & Zondervan
1663 Liberty Drive
Bloomington, IN 47403
www.westbowpress.com
1 (866) 928-1240

ISBN: 978-1-9736-3793-6 (sc)
ISBN: 978-1-9736-3794-3 (hc)
ISBN: 978-1-9736-3792-9 (e)

Library of Congress Control Number: 2018910194

Print information available on the last page.

WestBow Press rev. date: 11/14/2018

Contents

I AM WHOLE AND PERFECT AS I

WAS CREATED

I AM NOT MY BODY

I AM NOT MY ACCUMULATIONS

I AM NOT MY ACHIEVEMENTS

I AM NOT MY REPUTATION

I AM WHOLE AND PERFECT AS I

WAS CREATED

Dr. Wayne W. Dyer

To the Spirit of Abundance that is in each of you.

May you recognize your greatness

Discover your path

And make the contribution

You came to make.

Orin & DaBen

I dedicate this book to my parents Evelyn and Rudy Gordon. God knew me when he joined you two together. Between the two of you, there is high intelligence, creativity, talents, gifts and an abundance of love which I have acquired. Your multi-talented offspring is also your gifted child.

Thank you for Life!

Thank you for who You are to make me who I am!

Foreword

Harlem born Anna Gordon an African American woman whose life is anything but boring has a topsy-turvy blissfully blessed life that reveals itself in miraculous ways. Unmasking her deepest darkest secrets, she turns inward to reach for answers to life's dilemmas while living in a paradox of pleasure and pain, eventually reaching deeper into her complex yet witty mind, she comes face to face with herself, her true self a reflection of GOD.

These pages will take you on an interesting sometimes whimsical often quirky and humorous adventure as the "Memoirs of The Soul Searcher" gently unfold.

Anna and I have been friends for over 14 years. I never quite know when or how I will hear from her or where in the world her journey will take her next. I love and marvel at how easy it is for her to trust and follow her Spirit!

Infinite Blessings & Light!

Alexis Scott

The Introduction of ME!

I am a lover, a giver, and a peacemaker. These words I have heard over and over in my little head since I was a child. My spirit heard these words regularly. It can only be that God planted who I am in me with a voice. In other words, hearing those attributes continually and becoming them. Walking in my purpose; loving on people; giving to strangers and making peace with all men as a child; as a teenager; and as an adult.

Lots of pain and tears come with these characteristics because certain people of this world abuse and take advantage of kindness and generosity which they confuse with weakness and fear.

I cried a lot.

I grew up in Spanish Harlem, also known as East Harlem or El Barrio, where a melting pot of Blacks, Puerto Ricans and Italians resided. I lived in the projects which ran from 124th Street and Second Avenue to 118th Street and Franklin D. Roosevelt Drive, also known as FDR Drive. I loved my neighborhood. It always seemed like something was going on there like street fairs, basketball games, parades, and riots. Yes, the riots! Riots broke out occasionally with one of the clans. To my family and me, that was just another form of entertainment while watching them rumble with fists and sometimes knives from our apartment window. I remember my mom use to tell us to turn out the lights and get the binoculars.

In New York, the most popular way to get around was public transportation. Between the buses and trains operating on a 24/7-hourly schedule, I was never inhibited at all going place to place. I frequented both ways of traveling as often as I could to see something new like museums, zoos, aquariums, Broadway, Rockefeller Center, Statue of Liberty, Empire State Building, Wall Street and beaches to name a few. Living in Manhattan was overwhelming and breathtaking at times because nothing ever stopped or closed, and this is why it is called the city that never sleeps or The Big Apple. Although those days seemed adventurous and exciting, I always wanted more and living in New York allowed me to dream of other places and countries that I knew one day would come true by traveling abroad.

My grandfather was an amazingly creative and self-taught man who could build anything from scratch. He would tell me tales about his journeys traveling from the South to New York that would grip my attention for hours. I found myself visualizing him in his 1954 midnight blue Buick riding with my grandmother through the Carolina's, Virginia, Maryland and stopping off in Pennsylvania to see his brothers who had decided that Pennsylvania was as far north as they were going to go. After resting there, he kept on trucking until he reached his destination, New York City. Those stories I will never forget because they were my first inspiration, a real inspiration to go places I had never gone before. Listening and taking heed to my grandfather's stories were intriguing to me and I knew then that they were real, and I could make my dreams become reality as well. When I was in high school, my grandfather who had been suffering from asbestos lungs having only 3 percent of lung capacity, took a turn for the worse. No more storytelling. After his demise, a few years later I departed and moved to California, 3,000 miles away.

My new adventure was perfect to get a chance to go someplace new. I continued to raise my children there. Exploring places in San Diego County like San Ysidro, Chula Vista, Del Mar and La Jolla was a wonderful experience.

After that life changing experience in California, we moved back to the East Coast. I decided to go back to school to become a massage therapist. Being two years into my profession, I began studying eastern techniques like Shiatsu and Shiatsu Shin Tai which focused on meridians, acupressure and releasing of fascia which mainly affects the connective tissue. Then the ultimate opportunity presented itself when I met an affluent client, who unbeknownst to me, would later invite me to go home with her. I facilitated healing to her every week for one year using my eastern techniques combining them with my western modalities. She began to heal; her headaches subsided; her muscles and tissues started feeling subtle and regained energy, and her blood started circulating with ease. She was so pleased that she asked me to come and live with her on the other side of the world. I could not believe my ears, but it was true. I was about to go to the other side of the world...wow! My greatest anticipation had arrived. For the first time, I will be leaving the country. For the first time, I will be traveling first class on a double-decker airline. For the first time, I will be traveling in the air longer than five hours. For the first time, I have a passport and a visa. I am traveling abroad.!

In 2007, my dream to travel abroad became real. Living abroad, I began to blog, write short stories and poetic phrases about me. My life took a 180-degree turn. I began exploring me, teaching me, experimenting with me to find out who I was. Whatever was going on in my head, I wrote about it.

The Middle East was so different from my home. All homes were unique and architecturally designed creating exquisite beauty about them. I was living in one of these estates with my client and her family. The first five weeks I was there, I was ushered around by my client who introduced me to so many relatives and friends on different occasions. I was given beautiful gowns for me to wear to family weddings. It was nothing like anything I had ever seen in my life. On one occasion, we went to the desert where they had built two-story bungalows. The place was their get-a-way when the five families of the clan would come together to have fun and dine. Dining was always a smorgasbord of delicacies, fruits, and meats. They truly treated me like a princess. I felt so very special.

Because of the networking that my client administered for me, I was traveling around in incredible looking vehicles, working as a massage therapist traveling from home to home facilitating healing to many. So many people began to feel my touch, and many people became repeated clientele. I became a household name amongst her family and others. I felt so blessed and honored to get a privilege like this. During the three years I lived abroad; I got a chance to travel. I saw many wonders to behold, places on the planet that you only see on the cable channel. I witnessed diverse cultures and places venturing to Jeddah, Doha, Jakarta, and Bali in Indonesia to name a few. I took a trip to Cairo and rode a horse around the Giza Pyramids.

Growing up in New York started me on this incredible journey where I started seeing. Seeing my dreams of traveling abroad to places I only watched on TV or saw in the movies. These dreams manifested and came to life.

The joy of dreaming is something I hold dear to my heart with gentleness and certainty to believe and have faith that dreams do come true.

You will read about my many challenging, painful, awkward, crazy, angry, teary-eyed, humbling, happy and grateful moments I have divulged on paper.

Anna Elena Gordon

Memoirs of The Soul Searcher is a compilation of the lover, the giver, the peacemaker, the encourager and the healer God has blessed me to be.

I pray that I will bless you and inspire you to go through whatever life brings your way. To find your destiny and purpose in life is not always easy. It takes hard work. It takes guts. It takes persistence and most of all it takes discipline. Take the first step and search for the hidden dimensions of your life.

You will be astonished at what you find.

Peace and Blessings to You

Change

Change is the very fabric of one's existence. If there is no change, no growth, no quality of life, no peace within can evolve. So many people are bound because they think that they are stuck. So many miserable and unhappy people in the world because they don't understand that change is what brought them to where they are. Their choice in life; their decisions became their reality by the choice of change. You say, "I will do this or that…" it causes change. Or you say, "I will stay here or go there…" it causes change. If you say, "I want to be the greatest, yet you tell yourself you want to stay where you are…" again you changed your condition. So many people fear this word change because it unravels the unknown. It demands that you do something you might not have ever done before.

SCARED…. AFRAID…and allowing FEAR to begin to envelop your soul and your brain keeps telling you that it is not safe to change because your brain is protecting you and likes your complacency because it is safe. Your central nervous system (CNS) gets into the sympathetic mode where it gets on edge because now you want to change. So, you disturb your comfort zone; you disturb your complacency; you disturb your sleeping weakened spirit. You must be fierce to change; you must be courageous to change; you must want change so bad that your mind can't rest, and you become uneasy when change is demanding you to release it, so you can find who you are. NOW, your spirit is getting stronger; now you are

Anna Elena Gordon

becoming the man and woman that God intended you to be, your very purpose in life is unraveling itself and becoming visible to you. YOU are beginning to delve into the unknown where life will truly begin for you. CHANGE is a marvelous word that embarks on so many levels of life. Begin with the one thing that will make change and circumstances real. YOUR MIND is where it begins, in your MIND. "As a man thinketh, so is he" and so he becomes.

The Great Anticipation

02/26/07

The great anticipation had arrived. Still no butterflies - still nothing. First time I am leaving the country. The first time I will be traveling on a plane longer than a 5-hour flight. First time for a passport and visa as well. Today I am going abroad.

My airplane ticket was scheduled to leave on February 25th, but due to the inclement weather, a snowstorm dropped about 5 to 10 inches of snow in Maryland and the surrounding areas. It's just as well. I got to spend more time with my family.

The following day, I got dropped me off at the airport approximately 5 hours before takeoff. Everything went smoothly. Checked in my bags, found my gate then found a place to eat. One of the airport's security transportation guards did a double take and decided to chit chat with me the entire time I was eating. After casual conversation, I finished my lunch, and he went his way. While I was waiting to board, I decided to contact my family.

At last, the time had come to board. We shuttled to the airplane where I walked up to the second level to first-class seating. I had never traveled first class, so this was a treat. I was fed very well from the time we departed at 6 pm on February 26th to the time we arrive at 7:15 pm on February 27. The flight was indeed a long flight.

Upon my arrival, two men greeted me; one of which was holding a sign with my full name on it. My last name was spelled wrong, but who cared! It was my name. I felt special again. It was obvious that they did not speak English too well. The important words that was shared was passport and ticket for my bags. They took my one carry-on and started walking like we were in a race. We approached a counter where men in military uniforms verified my passport; stamped the visa and off we went sprinting through the airport. One man took the baggage tickets and proceeded to get my luggage. I was told to follow the other guy. We soon entered the parking lot where he motioned with his hand for me to wait while he took about 5 minutes to retrieve the vehicle. Once we met up with the other man and my luggage, we left the airport. It was dark. The ride to the house was about 1/2 hour. Not too much to see. I noticed a strip of car dealerships, brand named stores like Best – for Best Buy; signs on stores, road signs…all in a foreign language.

Upon arrival to the house, an entourage of ladies greeted me. One of the servants ushered me to my room which was on the ground level. It was a rectangular room with a bathroom having a toilet, sink, and shower. Nothing fancy, but cozy. Beige walls, beige blinds with an air conditioning unit under it. Opposite my large twin size bed were closets and shelves. There was a small quaint looking chair and matching ottoman adjacent to my bed diagonal on the corner wall.

Everyone was busy doing something which was standard. I went back to mainly stay in the kitchen while many servants greeted me introducing themselves. I asked to make a phone call. One of the assistants took me down this long hall, where I saw this huge room called the salon with boxes everywhere. (Come to find out that all my client's boxes had arrived that day by boat from the US where we met). One of my daughters was on her way to work, so I kept the conversation brief letting her know that I arrived and asked her to call everyone letting them know I was safe.

Wednesday, I was summoned by my client to have lunch with her. The lunch was an assortment of foods and drinks. After lunch, I went back to my room and took a nap. My client informed me that I would be going with her to meet her mother and afterward we were going to the farm until Friday.

While at her mother's house, we sat in a large sitting room. Her mom is a petite woman could be in her 70's. As we entered, my client greeted her mom first with a kiss on top of her head then greeted the other elderly ladies there who were either a friend of the family or a relative. Passively the room became full of sisters, nieces, cousins, and in-laws of all women. Servants brought in teas and coffees. Oops, cannot forget the little people. Five, 10 and I believe 13 were their ages. They were loquacious! Other little people arrived, again little girls ages eight months and two years old. After much conversation, we adjourned from that room and proceeded to go through a hallway to a huge lobby to another room where round tables strategically were set up which seated 6 to a table. The food prepared was a buffet-styled which was simply delicious. After dinner, we all went back to the sitting room, and incense was brought out in some urn for all to fan in front of them and put it into their hair and clothes. This ritual got rid of any food smells; again, much conversation. Then I was asked by my client's sister to come and speak with her about her arm. She is having chronic pain to the point that she is wearing a brace on her wrist. We spoke and set up my first appointment with her for a therapeutic massage. Shortly afterward, my client got up and started kissing all good bye-again starting first with her mother.

Once leaving her mother's house, we headed to the farm for two days. The farm is a place the family retreats to in the desert. It took approximately 45 minutes to get there. Oops, again I did not mention the custom-made Maybach I rode in going to her mother's house. Now, going to the farm, I was chauffeured in a custom-made

Anna Elena Gordon

Mercedes! Once we arrived at the farm it was late, so we were all given rooms to accommodate each of us. I roomed together with a friend of the family. The house was huge. It had doors leading to separate lofts and bedrooms. I was in one of the lofts with a spiraling staircase leading into the living room with three huge windows stretching arose the entire room. To the side of it was another open room with two full-size beds and closets on the one wall; a full bath as well. All bathrooms had a bidet.

The following morning was a wonder to behold. The grounds were gorgeous. We were in the desert where the sand is pink coral. Other guests had arrived and stayed the entire day, and of course, a much bigger spread served. This banquet style had at least 15 different dishes with the deserts and fruits on another table. Once the feast was over the guests left. My time clock had adjusted to theirs, so I was awake until 3 am. I got up at 8 am on Friday morning and laid around because no one was up but me. Ten o'clock rolled around, and I began to do my yoga. After my exercises, I got dressed and walked the perimeters of the grounds. I did this twice. One time was equivalent to a football field. After speed walking, I came back to my loft and took a nice long shower and ate a light lunch. It was a short retreat which only lasted the weekend.

Then what a treat! I was chauffeured back to the house all by myself in this custom-made beauty to behold Maybach which was forest green exterior and plush camel color interior where the back of the car was so long that I stretched out and my feet still didn't touch the front seat.

WOW!

What a welcoming!

Five weeks of working almost around the clock was exhausting. I became nocturnal working, eating and living against my normal clock. I would wake up at 7 or 8 in the morning and a few times at 9, depending on if anyone wanted to book a session with me starting at 1 or 2 in the morning for three hours. I was extremely exhausted. I had nothing else to give. My body felt drained. I returned to the USA after five weeks with such a feeling of gratitude and accomplishment. Little did I realize that this journey across the seas was just a glimpse of my future for the next three years.

The Guest Speaker

Sunday Afternoon

Graduation Ceremony!

WOW! I had committed to speak at my alma mater, regardless that I had become extremely ill after my return from being abroad.

I did speak though and got a standing ovation.

The words came from my heart and my spirit.

My speech was a healing experience to others and myself revealing that this was not about me. I let me go of my acute pain and spoke about my incredible experiences and adventures abroad. The gift to me was to those who attended and was present to hear. I enjoyed being the guest speaker giving my testimony about how grand life is when you follow our passion.

What You Read from This Point on Is....

Saturday, August 18, 2017

Okay, I need to start writing these things down. I am hoping that by revealing certain personalities, the reading of this book will inspire many.

I don't know when it started, but I do know that I have been talking to myself for quite some time now. Now I have never discussed this with anyone, and I have never asked a person who speaks to themselves to explain it. I know that I can be anywhere in my house by myself doing whatever-like today. I was eating watermelon facing the window being seated at the dining room table. VOICES… VOICES…VOICES…and then I read this:

"You need not leave your room. Remain sitting at your table and listen. You need not even listen, wait. You need not even wait; learn to become quiet, and still and solitary. The world will freely offer itself to you to be unmasked. It has no choice; it will roll in ecstasy at your feet." Frank Kafka

Stillness is the first requirement for manifesting our desires because in stillness lies our connection to the field of pure potentiality that can orchestrate an infinity of details for you." Deepak Chopra.

Every day – "Today I shall judge nothing that occurs."

Every day – "Meditate for 30 minutes in the morning and 30 minutes in the evening."

"You accept a thing as they are not as you wish they were in this moment. This moment is exactly the way it should be. Accept it."

I see myself evolving. My thoughts, my actions, my physical self is all opening up to accept me for where I am now.

Pain

Pain. The assimilation associated with pain brings on traumatic circumstances dealing with an emotional roller coaster.

Pain can bring you to tears, anger, anxiety, frustration, darkness, despair, hurt, numbness, lifelessness, shaking, disturbance, hate, dizziness, and loneliness. But, pain can also bring you awareness, clarity, creativity, absorption, peace within, soul-searching and serenity. Yeah, pain can do all this once you figure out which way you want to take it. Pain can be your enemy or your friend. Pain can be your downfall or your uprising. Pain can be an opening into your new venture in life bringing spontaneous responses within the universe and all that it has to offer. I know this might sound like, "what in tarnation! My pain is becoming unbearable, and I feel like I'm immobilized." But my beloved, that is the side where you allowed the pain to hit you the hardest. Trust me it happened to me. Let me tell you a little story.

Pain did become unbearable and almost immobilizing the summer of 2007 after coming back from the Middle East. It was so excruciating that I thought that I was going to lose it. The pain was severe to the point that I did not even associate with my family and those of you who know me know that my family is a BIG part of my world. This pain took my senses and wrapped them around an endless time frame of anger, self-pity, warpedness and weirdness of the mind.

Anna Elena Gordon

This pain thought that it was going to beat me up and tear my body and mind apart. No matter what I did, seeing a doctor and chiropractor the pain grew more and more in control of my being-like taking possession. I couldn't talk about it, couldn't sit, couldn't stand, couldn't walk, couldn't crawl, could lift, bend, turnabout or squat without this pain.

Then once I got tired of being tired of being tired of this calamity of anguish, I took a hold of myself. Something happened deep down inside of me where I had the feeling that if I didn't do something, anything, I wasn't going to last long. I focused on meditating and reading about pain and its side effects. I started reading about the mind and the molecular structure of emotions-hence pain. I started to take yoga classes (an hour by car each way). I started wearing orthotics to help me walk balanced. I found out that my flat footedness was causing some of this pain in my knees. This new me began to strengthen my weakness bringing out the side in me that has never given up- no matter what. I am a survivor! I am a warrior! I am a fighter! No longer will I allow this monster to chain me down. The shackles MUST come off. I had to show the pain that I was more than a wimp allowing it to control my exhausted self. This regime of newfound exercises and stretches with meditation and stillness started allowing my body and mind to overcome. I started feeling like me again. My inhales and exhales slow. My heart beating at its regular pace again. The stiffness in my joints felt lubricated and alive again.

I AM ALIVE...I AM SINGING...I AM SEEING ME AGAIN THAT I LONGED FOR FOR SO LONG.

You know, when you are in pain it feels like an eternity; like never-ending clusters of a vicious tormenting cycle. I decided to take on this pain I described. I became more creative in my thinking, more aware of my journey in life, enlightened to the point that I am a new one within.

So, I dare say to you, bear it. Bear the pain with the result being the optimist of what pain can do. Do not allow the pain to engulf and transform your livelihood into a permanent monster from the abyss. Sure, you might go through that in the beginning and the middle of this long endurance of a season, but once you take a hold of it you CAN, and you WILL come out like gold. The Bible says that God will never put any more on you than you can bear. Well, that only applies if you want to come out of it. Some people don't want to come out of their grueling circumstances, so they wallow in their misery.

I know you though, I know who reads my blogs and I am telling you this, my beloved, you can come out, you can go through the storm being victorious in the end. Our destiny and our faith is where we shine and become the light in the darkness that so many people fall victim.

I love you

Anna Elena Gordon

The Beginning

I need to write because I need to release. I want to write because I am missing something in my life. I need to write because I need to express myself without interruption.

Some of the most satisfying and fruitful times in life for me is being a mother. I have birthed and am raising two generations of children who are all unique and scrupulous. People respect, admire, adore, trust and believe in them because of who they are.

They are my branches that I have had the pleasure of sprouting from my tree. My tree had no real purpose until they arrived bringing life and beauty into my roots. My tree then had to be firmly replanted by the water which has given it substance and depth that only the water can. You see, being planted by the water, I must be strong, tenacious, and willing to be pushed, tugged, beaten when the elements and forceful presence of nature hurl at me. Because I have planted my tree by the water, my branches have grown and have survived what the elements of life have brought their way as well. There is nothing that my tree cannot withstand.

What makes my tree more beautiful is that now my branches have little branches sprouting from them. Oh, what joy it is to see my tree blossom. God has fulfilled his promise to me and that much more.

One of my branches is still very young but is holding on and learning to be strong like the other branches are.

Had I known the struggles, the tenacity, the endurance, the strength, the hurt, the tears, the beauty and unconditional love it took to plant my tree by the water, I would have made my tree even stronger by having more branches.

Trust

Trust – to firmly believe in the reliability, truth and the ability of someone or something.

Trustworthy – honest, truthful and reliable.

Where are these people? I ask you, where are they? They don't exist! And, if they do, most of them are hiding. Somewhere in the depths of the remote parts of the earth where they stay because they know that they are safe there. I feel I need to go there sometimes, away from all the pessimistic and hypocritical people.

All my life, I have been this word. All my life being this word has caused me grief because being this word you become a loner. People use you and take you for granted when you trust. I am once again disturbed because of this word. I just recently found out that the TRUST I had in a certain individual has tarnished and violated me and mine. Once again, I trusted and once again I was disappointed to know that the trust I relied on was an imposter.

Why can't people be good? Why can't people be honest? Why can't people tell the truth ALL the time? I have been questioning myself about this all my life. And you know what, I still don't know the answer. Yeah, yeah, yeah, I know that it all started in the garden of Eden after that heinous episode and resulting in deception and corruption in the brain. But that is no excuse for me being the way that I am. Why can't I find others like me? I raised my four to be trustworthy and trusting they are staying that way. Liars are my pet peeves. Can't stand them. Lying serves no purpose, and it appears that the world is getting worse. But in the meantime, I can only hope and pray that what I see is temporary. I am an optimist, and I believe that someday soon the world will rid itself of the untrustworthiness of humanity. Honesty, truth, reliability is the way to go. For those who can't see the big picture, unfortunately, no good will come your way.

So, I say, STOP to all of them that can't handle the truth. STOP to all that are liars and warped minded individuals who have no future for the good of humanity.

Peace

First Real Friend

I'm working on maintaining discipline with my logging. I hear it all the time, "Write Anna write it down" and then I hear it again, "You need to start writing things down Anna so that you can reflect on these days."

Did I mention my friend? Hmmm.

Well, I met this lovely Chinese Canadian woman the beginning of January. I was compelled to go to the bookstore. The voice was loud and clear. So, I obeyed, and when I got there, I realize that I had been in this place before. I remembered not ever going upstairs. So, this is where I would venture today. There was a children's section of arts and crafts, toys and books. I wondered around there exploring all the diverse things that the bookstore had for ages from toddlerhood to grade level. I was looking for paints and brushes and an easel. I didn't find them, so I started towards the other side of the second floor to the adult books. Then, oh my goodness. Nature was calling in a very strong and loud way. I started looking at the self-help books on growth, appearance, healing, etc. I also was checking out the people. Then I spotted a little lady that appeared to have such a sweet spirit. I asked her where the bathroom was. She kindly directed me, and off I went. After my major release, I headed back to the same location and found this little lady first off. We spoke as if we had known each other for years; even had similar interests. My new-found friend was one of the head nurses at the hospital. I had also noticed that she had purchased the book, "Power of Now," that I was anticipating on getting myself. Come to find out that the author was a personal acquaintance of hers. So of course, she encouraged me to get it and then gave me a gift of a yin-yang symbol bookmarker. We exchanged numbers, and I knew then that I had found a real friend of like-mindedness and that I would be spending a great deal of time with her in this far away land we were both visiting. She is one of the few people that I have been praying to meet. Now I had someone to really talk to.

This Time Is All There Is

I was sitting here checking out all of Myspace correspondence (does this still exist?) of my kids; reading the blogs; reading the comments and feeling good.

I am in a place right now where time is all there is. No family, no driving, no movies, no bathtub, LOL. I have access to a bathtub, but it's down a long hall. Only me, my music, my DVD's and my books. As of lately massaging has been sporadic. Go figure! I come all the way to the other side of the planet, and the mentality is the same about my profession, hah-very seasonal. Anyway, time is all there is. Living in the Middle East makes me think a lot. Being by myself is making me think a lot. Having no one to talk to when I want to share makes me THINK a lot. This time is all there is. I am rambling now because I am writing what is coming to my head. Sometimes there is a lot of turbulence going on upstairs and sometimes the peace that surpasses all understanding ripples like the waves in an ocean-very serene. Sometimes the stillness I experience in the early morning while I am sitting by the pool surrounded by nothingness is life-changing. Time is all there is!

Time is all there is and if I had to do it all over again…God is with me no matter where I go, and He is always telling me, this time is all there is…for now.

So, enjoy the moments of solitude to appreciate your inner voice. Enjoy the quietness because that is the only way you can hear God and yourself. The Bible says that no matter what situation you are in one should be content. Learning that statement isn't that easy for me. I have to turn the loudspeaker down that is occasionally playing in my head. Then I learned it…the peace, the joy…the stillness, the happiness in knowing that this time is all there is. Be still and know that I am BEING. Peace

My Hair

Why is it that every time I want to talk about my hair, my words get erased! This paragraph is the third time I am writing about my hair. What in the world is going on?

Okay, let's start again. Hmmm, maybe I started writing the wrong things or something. So, I will attempt to be nice and voice my opinions about my hair in another fashion.

I love my hair, believe it or not. My hair was so long when I was little. I could reach it by putting my hands up my back and holding it. Yep. The problem with my thick long hair growing up in the 50's was that there were NO conditioners. You heard me, no conditioners. Can you imagine the pain I went through? The headaches from combing my hair when it dried. Oh, my goodness. There was no mercy or empathy from my mother or older girl cousins when it came to my hair. After they washed it, they just let it dry on its own then decided to comb it and brush it. Oh, the pain I experienced was unforgettable not to mention the fact that it was downright unbearable. Whew! Excruciating. I used to get migraines sometimes. I made such a raucous that my hair only got washed and pressed once a month. Trust me, when that time came once a month, I dreaded it. I said all that to say this…I still love my hair even if I am bald-it is starting to grow back, hah. I love the texture, and I love the color. My salt and pepper hair is all over now. That is why I have been stripping my hair white for the last maybe 4 or so years. I love white hair. I think it looks fabulous. So, me of course with my impatient self decides to go white instead of waiting for my season to arrive. This last time was it though. Coming to the Middle East with white bleached hair was not a good idea. Matter of fact, coming to Middle East with any hair is not a good idea. The water eats it away. You see, the water comes from the deep trenches in the belly of the desert where it is so hard that it dries your hair out to the point of breakage. Few women out here only wash their hair once every two weeks and when they do they use bottled water to preserve its strength, (this is what I heard). So, a hard lesson learned for me, huh?

BALDNESS! Well actually, this isn't the first time I had become bald. Come to think of it this might be my fourth time. I am sure if you ask my kids they will know for sure. I am always messing with my hair or someone else is always messing with my hair and before you know it chop-chop clipper time!

But, I do love my hair. Me and my hair have gone through a lot of good times and not so good times. My hair is very strong. Thank God, lol! Now I can't wait for it to grow back. This time, I think I will have a perm- short one.

I Need a Break

YEAP!

I need a break. It is time to come home. You know, about five months ago I started meeting people from the United States. Started hanging out with them occasionally and having fun. Going to their compounds, eating REGULAR foods, listening to nice music-the whole nine yards. I WAS HAVING FUN! But, I don't think that was such a good idea. I mean, it has had two different effects on me. One is what I just described and the other being that by doing those things it has made me a little homesick.

I like traveling and doing my thing. I like being able to see whomever whenever and can't do that out here. Although this side of the world is the "bomb" when it comes to shopping at the malls and purchasing things you would never see in the States, the bottom line is that that is all there is.

What I miss most is the freedom and the creativity and the exploring. This place doesn't offer me that. No freedom to get up and walk to the corner store for a snack or go to the movies or a theatre, there aren't any. No real radio stations to listen to smooth jazz or comedian talk shows in the mornings. No amusement parks with the munchkins, no sitting at the parks, there aren't any, no freedom to hang out at the beach- no beaches or go to your neighbor's home to visit. I can't just call my family without it being connected to the dispatch or central, as they call it, where all might be listening or if I call on my mobile phone the cost becomes outrageously expensive. Why? I am in the Middle East, on the other side of the planet.

I am ready to come home. I miss talking with my family mainly my children who I talked to practically every day. I miss my grandchildren and their precious selves. Believe it or not, I miss driving. I miss the Amtrak going to see my mom and visiting my pops. I miss my country.

You know, I got it pretty good out here. God has blessed me to be with a very distinguished affluent family, and that is a cool thing to experience, but you know, after being amongst them and seeing exactly how they live life with their family, I'm getting an eye full, and I am ready to come home. I am planning this very long airplane ride back to the states in July because I don't want to miss my oldest grandchild's birthday. Then I will be home until the end of August. I will return here until my spirit tells me my season is up. I am working on some exciting new things and new places to go out here when I return.

But, for now, I need a BREAK.

Anna Elena Gordon

Topsy-Turvy

Sometimes I feel like this. Sometimes I have no idea what I am doing. Sometimes going with the flow is all I know. Who do I turn to when things become topsy-turvy in my life, GOD! Okay, but sometimes I need someone tangible to have conversations. Like now, I feel like I don't know what to do. I put myself in situations that I think are positive until something happens that didn't work or last too long.

Sometimes I feel like I have a split personality. I hear this one loud voice most of the time while I am walking in the mornings, while I am trying to read not fully comprehending the words on the pages. It takes some time for my mind to focus while it starts contemplating multiple things at once or even when I am trying to process a major decision I must address. There is another loud voice talking about past situations, talking about what if's, talking about the mess that I don't want to hear. Am I going crazy? Am I losing it? I have been dealing with these other voices in my life for a very long time now. I mean since I was a young adult. Who is it? Reading some books suggest that it is my ego, my subconsciousness, my fear, my childhood darkness. Whichever one it is, I can't take it anymore, and I want it to go away! Sometimes one of the voices get so loud that the only way I can sometimes still it is to go into a meditative state. Most of the time this loud voice does nothing but dwell on the negative and the fear. It has conversations with me without any response. It just talks and talks, and I try very hard to disconnect it and at times I am successful, but only for a short while. I have noticed that I go into a zone which takes me to the past, and then I get emotional, and that is when the voice gets louder. But let me ask you something, can one stay conscious all the time? I mean, I hear people talking about stuff like this. I am reading a lot of self-help spiritual guidance books that suggest that it can happen, but does this happen all the time? If these voices are coming from me, living in a subconscious state in the past, then I want OUT. I want to be aware in the present and in the moment where God is all the time; where peace and joy is all of the time. I am noticing that while I am writing these words, I don't hear the loud voice. I don't even know what gender it is. It sounds like me, and sometimes it doesn't, it talks to me, and sometimes it doesn't and expects me to listen to it. It is always telling me things which are suspect. But what if they are the wrong things? How did I distinguish the difference between these loud voices? To whom am I listening? Could this be my subconsciousness trying to get out? Could this be my spirit trying to soar like the eagle I want to be? Which voice should I be listening? Again, how am I supposed to know! They say that the first voice you hear is from God or your spirit or your intuition. But, I hear them most of the time. So, what is that?

I feel like I am being pulled and pushed like someone is playing tug of war with my mind that is supposed to be on straight. How in the world did I make it this far in life with these loud voices going on inside my head? I don't know why I can't explain myself the way I want to? Why can't I remember things I read and see and hear and feel? Did something happen to me at birth? Why do I feel like I am on the outside of me looking in – PRACTICALLY ALL OF MY ADULT LIFE PEOPLE.

Topsy-turvy…yeah, this is a spooky thing that I am going through right now. I feel imprisoned in this adult body. The body is growing, but the mind is standing still. I listen to my children, and I know for certain that they know more than me. That is depressing. Why can't I remember things?

I need help with this because at this time in my life I can't seem to do it by myself. I have tried God; I have tried reading; I have tried educating myself. I want a simple explanation to ME or at least some thoughts about this.

I Want

I want someone to take care of

I want someone to take care of me

I want to love a man again

I want to hold and caress a man again. Not any man but my man forever and ever

I want to live to be able to see my grandchildren grow up

I want to live to see my great-grandchildren grow up

I want my parents to live until they are a century plus in their right minds

I want to live to be a century plus in my right mind

I want to live a full life

I want to travel all over the world

I want to be a philanthropist

I want to have a successful and prosperous business

I want to build a legacy for my children's children and family

I want to hear God's voice all the time

I want to be free in mind, body, and soul

I want I desire I need to have these things come to past

I want to be happy

I want to love someone who understands me most of all

But what I want is for me and mine to continue to be healthy prosperous and loving to all that encounter us.

That will make the difference in my life.

I want…. what do you want?

You Are

You are a special, unique person and you have a meaningful contribution to make to the world. Every person is born with a purpose. There is a reason you are here; you have a role to play that no one else on the planet can fulfill. The special contribution you came to make is your predestined life's work. When you are doing that work, you are following your higher path, and your life will have joy, abundance, and well-being that follows you.

As you do what you love, money and abundance will flow freely to you.

Know who you are and live. The greatest miracle is life itself. You are the miracle, and you can create anything you want which is another great miracle. There are no barriers, no limits to what you can do and have. The only limitation is what you picture for yourself, ask for yourself, and believe for yourself.

Miracles are love in action.

You are!

Anna Elena Gordon

When the Door Shuts

When the door shuts…what to do?

This blog is about to mess with something higher than me because as I was writing it suddenly vanished! So, I will attempt to write this again.

When the door shuts, something is going on in the universal atmosphere that is incomprehensible but most definitely a certainty. When the door shuts, you must be still because movement will only create turbulence in your life.

When the door shuts, your mind goes places trying to comprehend reasoning, circumstances, LIFE, but there are no answers. When the door shuts, is like your soul your entire being is being compressed and sucked into a very dark place without any walls for security.

I felt helpless, mindless without my common sense searching for any answers trying to make sense out of the "why." My body became crippled; my mind became like a funnel of emptiness. I couldn't dance, I couldn't sing, I couldn't pray, I couldn't walk, I couldn't drive. Six months in desperation seeking answers from doctors, psychiatrists and through sleep studies, bi-polar testing, narcolepsy testing without any results.

What to do? What could I do? I was baffled. My common sense had left me, and without that, I felt vulnerable. The only thing I had left to do was give up. My salty tears were inevitable because of my condition. Pain from anguish thoughts roaming through my inner being.

When the door shuts, I have learned to allow it to shut and then peace will come. When I gave up the search for the "why", God intervened. He told me that I was in preparation. He told me that my experiences in life were not about finding the answers to the "why," but it was about being a testimony to others. He told me that I had a strong hold on me that was a generational bondage that gripped my very essence years ago-before my time. A bondage so obscure and deep that the only way to conquer it was to go through a metamorphosis of my spirit, mind, and body.

Once I gathered myself and harkened to His voice, I took heed immediately. Then and only then could I start doing the things that I loved so much like walking, singing, driving, praying and dancing. The battle within me was poisonous to my wellbeing. It had to go! Life would not exist had I not taken heed.

When the next door shut-and there have been a few since that first experience-I have realized that I am a conqueror and that this walk in life is not about me. Understanding that when the door shuts, I know without any doubt that there is another one opening for me.

Now when the door shuts, I wait and exhale effortlessly knowing that this path of mine is my journey…my destiny. I approach it gracefully with anticipation of the glory that will come from the knowing. The knowing that my GOD has it all worked out, and nothing will ever disturb my peace like that again when the door shuts, 'When the door shuts…what will you do?

Namaste

Anna Elena Gordon

Mother and Father

When I wake in the morning, I can see. I look up and say good morning to my Father. I check out the time and get on my sweats and go for a walk-a-bout with my Mother. I talk and walk with them both listening to the trees whistling at me telling me how good it is to see me. Listening to the birds singing their morning tunes to me. Sometimes I get a chance to say masala kar or salaam malekum to the grounds people. I walk around the grounds looking at the beautiful landscape that the men care for like it is their own. The men cleaned the pool on a daily. I look up at the bright clear sky which sometimes isn't so clear because of the sandstorm the night before. Then I start talking and singing while I'm walking. When I stop singing I can hear creativity flowing through me. I can feel the sun beaming on the rooftop of my cranial melting its way through my life's being, giving me energy. I can hear my spirit choosing my day for me, so I know what to expect. All in all, I accept all that my spirit is telling me with adoration and anticipation. I am loving me.

As I ponder the feelings and the thoughts that overtake me, I come to realize that who keeps me, who envelopes me, who breathes through me, who walks and talks with me, who shadows me, who protects me, who guides me, who loves me more than life itself is me. The miracle in that is my Father God, and my Mother Earth has done all this for me.

Father took Mother's dirt and made man's essence by breathing life into his nostrils; then took a rib from man, made from Mother's dirt to make me – a woman. Talk about intricate details. The simplicity of it all is astounding.

So, when I see and hear and walk and talk and sing and listen and understand that every breath I take is because someone loved me so much to breathe life into my nostrils through some dirt............. All I am saying is only my everlasting omniscient, omnipotent, heavenly Father and soulful earthly Mother has blessed me to be. They have allowed me to come into existence through my biological father planting a seed in my biological mother which brought forth creativity, beauty, love, compassion, integrity, and a pure heart, a liver, a stomach, a bladder, kidneys, a spleen, small intestines, large intestines, sinews, skeleton, muscles, tendons, ligaments, skin, eyes, nose, ears, mouth and a brain that can compute all this.............

Who can do all this to each human being on the planet? I'm not even mentioning our counterparts like the animals, birds, insect, rocks, volcanoes, fire, water, air, wind. Do you get my point? Who can do all this, but a divine higher being other than ourselves which is my Father, GOD! And to top it off, he gave us this and that much more to be able to do as much and more than he can; only dare to have the faith to believe it.

WOW, what an incredible journey to go truly where no man has gone before. To taste the glory of God and sit with Him while he tells me all that he wants me to be- since I can remember and to have the opportunity to now experience the beginnings of all that I have heard Him saying. WOW...who is God? Hey, I just gave you a glimpse of who He is to me. Just a glimpse. Hope you got the message.

Namaste

Anna Elena Gordon

The Gift of Life

All my life I have loved-especially children. Being the eldest of my two siblings, I started taking care of them at an early age. Those early times invited sibling rivalry, playing together being a parent when I was in charge and making decisions that didn't always get the popular vote. I loved the smell of babies; I loved changing diapers (at times); I loved their tiny clothes and hats, and shoes-and still do. Babies are adorable-I started calling them little people because they are just that -little people with a whole lot to offer.

Then I started having children, WOW! The feeling of carrying a child within my insides felt overwhelming at first. The physical, psychological and mental challenge that I went through became an awakening like no other. Belly growing looking like a huge basketball-sometimes even a football. Face swelling, feet swelling, hair growing rapidly along with the fingernails and toenails. Gaining crazy weight, having a bottomless pit (I never got full). All those precious times feeling life moving inside of me-growing bigger and bigger. Feeling little one's heart beat-walking like a penguin and duck-waddling horizontally because vertically was no longer possible. Nine months of topsy-turvy emotional imbalances from fatigue, headaches, upset stomach, itching, inflammation, toxemia, heartburn, discomfort, pelvic pain, regional lumber pain and mental frustration.

Then the moment of arrival-when labor starts. On my goodness. I thank God that the actual memory of labor pain is a blur when it's all over. But, during that time all calmness is gone. Excruciating, unbearable, inconceivable pain unlike any other pain in existence. A toothache, migraine, being punched, stubbing your toe, hitting your funny bone got nothing on labor pain. That pain is in a category all by itself. Then the push...whoa...the push that makes you feel like you are about to explode. The ultimate momentous journey into the breakthrough of your child about to come into this world. BAM! Out burst the newborn looking oblivious having slept through this entire incredible experience having no clue that the world awaits their glory.

Yes, his or her glory-their precious life that makes all the above bearable and with time allowing the same craziness to happen again and again and again!

So, then tell me, why in the world would you give up this precious little life, this little being that is truly the gift of life. Understanding that if you go through the entire emotional roller-coaster to bring him or her into this wonderful world shouldn't this time be honored? Shouldn't this time be a time of reflection, adoration, and admiration? A time only a mother can appreciate. A time when you have accomplished your greatest feat. A time when the world stands still for you to say, YES! You did this wondrous act all by yourself. A time to be proud. A time to pat yourself on the back in total adulation.

For me, the answer was yes...four glorious times.

Breezy

I am embarking upon a journey only God in his infinite wisdom could have allowed to come together like this. In my wildness imagination, my mind could not have conceived all that I am experiencing. Sure, I always thought that I was different. For years, I wondered why. Sometimes I still wonder-but not in dismay because I realize that I am who I am because my creation is what it is; an individual just like everyone else who knows this to be a fact. There are no clones. Everyone on the planet-even twins, triplets, quadruplets and so on are all individuals-make no mistake about it.

Being and knowing that I am different makes me excited and overwhelmed yet bewildered at times. I never did beat the same drum as others did or do now. I now accept my individualism to touch and reach others blessing them with my smile, my appearance, my attitude, my love, my giving, my appreciation for allowing them to be whoever they are around me.

I love me; therefore, I can love others.

I am feeling things I haven't felt in me before. My life is experiencing all this emotional bliss, and for the first time I feel exceptional and that exceptionalism I'm sure I passed on to my beloved children.

About a month ago one of my clients (who I was massaging) saw me with wings and called me an angel. WOW! That took me aback to the point of tears. She saw white wings on my back. Intuitive, clairvoyant whatever-this is who she is and what she saw.

My name Anna is international. My unique name being able to read it from the left or the right on paper is the same! That is amazing to me. It is German, French, Spanish, South African and some other places around the globe as well. In the Bible, Anna was a prophetess. She resided in a temple that she never left. She had a husband who passed on, and she never married again. The ultimate mission was where she would see The Christ. When the time came, she welcomed Mary holding The Christ in swaddling clothes into her temple to be circumcised and blessed. She spoke of prophetic things to come to past about him and then she was gone. The Bible speaks no more of her.

My life has some similarity to this Anna in the Bible. Now that I am a healer, I see it more and more. I still don't know all there is to know about me because the universe is rapidly flooding its gates with all I have need of exposing itself to me and sometimes I don't catch all of it on my surfboard riding the waves of eternity. But, when I do catch a glimpse and snatch some of me, I feel assured that finding all of me, who I am, is not so far away. I will see me as I am-soon very soon.

I have told my story to those who are close to me and to some who I feel understand, that I feel like I am another entity of myself. Not the mind, body and soul integration because that is one in me, but something different. Like I am looking at myself outside of myself-not like looking in a mirror but just with my eyes seeing me. I know I am me, and I can touch me, but I feel like I am outside of me. If that makes no sense to you, I thoroughly understand because trying to describe what I mean is complicated. All I know is that I am a complicated individual who is multitalented which intimidates many who don't take the time to know me, understand me or appreciate me and that is why I don't speak on a lot of things that I can do, but you know what? My attitude on that is changing. It's not boasting either- it is just ME and what the Creator has given ME. So why shouldn't I use these talents and gifts? Why shouldn't I show the world what God has given me? To lay them aside or let them lie dormant would mean to lose them and not appreciate God for my many gifts and talents and I can't allow that because that would mean that I don't appreciate all that I am! Well…this is about me anyway-not anyone else. I am expressing my thoughts about me, Anna, and who I am.

You know, I am going to write a book about me one day, and when I finish it, all will know the real me because I will be in completion… it's all about ME.

Catch me if you can, LOL, because God is moving me very fast. I do have wings, wings I have been seeing in my dreams for years flying high like an eagle overlooking mountainous ranges topped with snow. So, maybe these are the wings that young lady saw on my massage table. All I know is that my dreams, visions, premonitions are beginning to manifest into who I am and what I am doing and going to do. The day will come when I can see me and feel me inside of me not looking on the outside looking at me any longer. Then I will be free and entire wanting nothing. The multisensory Anna will awaken.

Again…this is ABOUT ME.

Namaste

Should I

Can I tell you what I'm thinking...can I share with you my thoughts...would you see me differently from expressing myself... will this make you uncomfortable...will my words separate us? Bottom line is that I have to say what I am feeling and the only way I know how to do that without fear is to write it on paper. Yeah, I am cautious right now because of what I am feeling for you. This emotion that won't let me rest is weighing heavily and continuously on my heart. The kind of feelings that I only get when I am about to go head-over-heels with my heart on someone.

No...no...no it doesn't happen like this very often when someone like you comes into my life-single, footloose and fancy-free AND on my birthday! The moment I saw you it was like...who are you? Your energy and your spirit is so alive and welcoming. Then you were introduced to me and your name. I have never met someone with your name before...and that face...what a smiley face with the brightest eyes. Then you sat down, and we spoke. WHOA! You gave me your card which would be the beginning of a wonderful relationship.

I had to call you...I just had to call you. I watched your card sit on my computer desk for a couple of days hearing it call me saying., "Pick me up and call me." Then I couldn't take it any longer, and I called. And guess what? You were hoping that I would call you too and of course, the rest is in the making.

But Mr. you are in my head all the time. Can't seem to stop thinking about you. I like being in your presence. I miss not hearing from you at least a few times during the week. I feel bashful calling you (and I'm not usually this way). There is just something about you where I don't want to let go. I don't know. It could be that what I am feeling for you-you don't feel for me…and that is okay. Truly! I just like being in your presence. I like your gentle voice. I like you cooking in the kitchen preparing food because "I'm worth feeding." I like us sharing our life stories. I like listening to your logic, wisdom and I love the way you make me laugh. When I am around you, I feel like I have escaped and gone where I haven't been in a very long time. I feel that I become ageless, just spending precious moments with you during a time and place where you only read in fairy tales. Oh, I don't know…I don't know where this is going. I know that I found a friend that I wish was a little closer so that I could spend more time. I have a difficult time calling because I don't want to displease you like coming on too strong or something. I don't want to run you off or away from me. I want us to be friends. I want to become something more, but we talked about our feelings and situations and the past relationships, and it is scary. My heart is racing towards this because this could be it, the big bang, but I feel afraid to pursue. My mind is stopping me because of our conversations and because I respect you for who you are. I respect the fact and knowing that you don't want to settle down. I respect the fact that you too are scared.

So, tell me Mr. what I should do? What I should do about these emotions inside of me giving me all kinds of feelings. Tell me please what you are thinking so that I can get a grip on myself.

Should I continue or should I not…so I can relax.

The Braces

This is 2007 and I have been a "gap sista" all my 53 years of life on this marvelous planet. From the time I can remember people always commented on my gap. Some would say that it was a mark of beauty; some would say that it meant that you lied a lot, and some would say that it was my personally-on and on went the remarks about my gap.

Well, for those who don't know, this is how the "critiqued gap" started. When I was an infant, toddler and elementary school-aged munchkin, I sucked my thumb. It was good to me, LOL. Tasted rather juicy and soft and was just the right size to make me feel very peaceful and happy. My thumb was my best friend when I was alone. It soothed me to sleep, assisted me while I was watching television and gave me hope when I felt sad. My thumb was "the joint."

I remember when my mother used to try and make me stop sucking my thumb. She tried using socks and tying my hands in them. I don't know when I stopped, but eventually, I did. I don't recall going through any withdrawals or anything, so I guess I released my thumb in love to do its other tasks. But, I do remember the results of sucking my thumb, and that was the GAP. Never really liked the way my two front teeth separated like bugs bunny.

Like I said, all my 53 years I have had this gap, so I decided that the gap had been around long enough, and it was time to go. I appreciated the gap and all its worldly criticisms and compliments coming from everyone, BUT me. But the gap's destiny has come to an end. I have said goodbye, and I watch it daily, getting smaller and smaller and smaller. HOW?

I GOT BRACES!!! Yes, siiiiirrrrreeeeeeee bob. Got braces about a month ago and love them! Kind of sensitive at times like in the beginning and my last visit to the dentist when the orthodontist tightened them again, but all in all I am seeing the gap disappear and loving it.

I must wear these braces for approximately eight months to a year, but so what. This itsy-bitsy time frame for my teeth to look beautiful to me is not that long a period. To me, it is worth every bit of cleaning with the special brushes and rinsing and flossing, etc. Those are just good habits anyway for taking care of my mouth.

Anyway, the gap is becoming no longer, and I am so ready to embrace each day until the braces are gone. I want to love me all over (which I do), but I was getting tired of putting my hands over my mouth when I laughed. Didn't do it always but did it enough. I want to laugh and have a beautiful smile for me. I am the one looking at me all the time, and I want to see me without a gap for the next 53 years of my ageless, healthy happy, beautiful life.

YYYYYYEEEEEEEAAAAAAAAAAAAAHHHHHHHHHH! LOL

I Can't Breathe

Is it that difficult to breathe through your mouth with your nose closed? Well, I had a hard time. Thought I was drowning in 10 inches of water above coral with the waves hitting me like they were spanking me.

Okay, okay let's start from the beginning. I went to Jeddah this weekend. The weather was lovely. I stayed in a hotel overlooking the Red Sea from the 9th floor. WOW! After checking in, we got our bathing suits on and headed for the beach which was about 40 miles north of the hotel. We get there and set up under an umbrella. My companions got their gear for snorkeling. I told them to go ahead because I just wanted to chill on my beach chair and finally become all one color. During the two hours we were there, at one point I got so hot I just had to get into the water. Now they told me that the coral was sharp especially by the shore, so I had to tiptoe like I was on eggshells into the water. Boy, the bottom of my feet was like "What in the world are you doing…go back; girl go back it hurts." But I was determined to get wet, so I kept going until I got about half my body wet and then I sat in the water. It was like bath water and clear as can be. After I soaked myself, I tiptoed back into the sand returning to my spot under the umbrella. A few minutes later my friends arrive, and we headed back to the hotel. Great time. They enjoyed their snorkeling admiring the beautiful colorful fish that one would only see in the Red Sea and I enjoyed becoming the

Anna Elena Gordon

same color. That evening we decided to go back to the beach club the next day, and this time I was going snorkeling.

Okay, I got up the next day and indulged myself next door at the 7-star palace hotel spa. I got a massage, a pedicure, a manicure and a mud wrap which lasted 4 hours! I went back to the room all excited about snorkeling. My friend and I went to the beach, rented snorkeling gear which included shoes (because of the sharp coral), fins and snorkel mask and proceeded towards the reef. Got into the shallow water and could hardly walk. The waves were hitting my body which was causing me to slip and slide on the slippery coral and rock formations. I was like, whoa! Then to top it off I couldn't get my fins on because I was being tossed to and fro. So, my friend held me while I was getting my fins on which didn't help my body from being tossed. LOL… my torso and legs going one way and my feet which were being held by my friend going another way. It was a sight to see, LOL. Okay now, the fins are on. Then I put my mask on. Time to go snorkeling. People, I put my face into the 10-inches of water, and the waves were so aggressive I almost thought I was downing. I gasped like I was drowning and couldn't catch my breath with only a face full of water. I COULDN'T BELIEVE IT! I was like "whoa," now I know I can breathe with my mouth…so I tried again. Okay, waves hitting me getting upset me because I couldn't enjoy them. I put my face under again and saw beautiful fish. It was amazing! Then suddenly after about 10 seconds of breathtaking wonders under the sea, I gasped again. Salt water got in my mouth; my body started falling and tumbling from the waves. I couldn't seem to catch my balance which caused water to rush into my nostrils. That was it. My friend said, "What's the matter? Just breathe through your mouth". So agitated I said, "I'm trying, but I can't seem to breathe through my mouth." I told him to go on and leave me. I departed from the water very annoyed at myself for not being able to #1 – stand in the water; #2 – get my fins on by myself; #3 – breathe through my mouth! What craziness!!

So, I ask you…is breathing through your mouth that difficult? YES, IT IS…LOL.

I really must learn how to snorkel. I'm going to get me a mask and practice in my pool! I'm going to learn how to breathe through my mouth if it's the last thing I do!

My Climbing Debut

I met a group of expats at a designated area, and we all climbed into vehicles that were assigned to us and off we went. We were on the paved road for about 20 minutes when suddenly, the driver turned off into a dirt road. This dirt road was heading out to somewhere looking like nowhere in the desert. We hit rocks and holes and was being tossed and stirred up like we were all on the Cyclone roller coaster in Brighton Beach, NY. I saw nothing in front of me but never-ending dry brown dusty dirt. Finally, in the near distance after about another 20 minutes other vehicles were parked at obviously the destination point where a caravan of vehicles was now camping. In the interim, about 15 vehicles eventually showed up. We all signed in and acquainted ourselves which took about an hour. First timers, like myself, had to get into this circle in the middle of everyone else to introduce ourselves. There were 8 of us from all over the globe giving a very brief introduction – name, occupation and lifetime in the Middle East.

Shortly after that, you hear a cowbell ringing…low and behold it was 4 o'clock, time to go on the hike of the day. We all took off like a stampede heading for the landmass. As we neared the edge of the mountain, it appeared like the people in front of me were falling off the cliff-everyone before me started disappearing. The ground at the edge went vertical. What a drop! I was like…what! Are we going straight down there? The stampede of expats was moving down this rocky formation like it was a plateau. As I started down holding onto loose rocks for dear life that were beside me and stepping on rocks beneath me, about 5 minutes down my knees started acting up. GOOD GRIEF! I thought I was in shape. HAH, now I knew that I was not. Not only was this drop steep but there was no trail to follow. We all were on our own. It was dangerous, but also exciting and exhausting. These rock formations and dunes was quite the adventure before me. We descended vertically three more times and plateaued three times before coming to which looked like the end of the world. There was nothing in front of this edge but space. We were at the top of one of the highest peaks in the world looking down into this dark abyss. WOW! It was breathtaking. We were on top of the mountain where the earth just stopped becoming.

This spot wasn't exactly a rest stop, but believe you me, I and a few others HAD to collect ourselves. I was panting, and my cardiovascular system was working overtime. WHEW! After drinking some water and taking pictures, we turned around and was now heading back up the other side of the mountain which was as vertical going up as it was coming down. I was like…I'm not going to make it… I'm not going to make it. As it was, my little knees were screaming at this point. They were tiring and about to give way. My legs hadn't felt this much endurance in quite some time. All my efforts: my lungs, my heart, my arms and legs, knees and feet were collaborating like never before to make it up this never-ending mountain. Off I went realizing about a quarter of the way up that it took more of my efforts to get back on top of the plateau. Now my legs started shaking. WHOA…sweat was becoming profusely obvious and the pulling up, holding on and scrambling on these loose rocks up this steep vertical cliff was like fighting a war! I was at war with my body parts, and my panting became louder and louder. My throat became dryer and dryer. I had to stop a couple of times to drink some water which didn't do a thing.

Remember when Sméagol, the Gollum, was climbing up that steep mountain leading the way in The Lord of the Rings? Well, imagine me climbing something like that.

I made it to the halfway point and there waiting for me, and the others was a barrel filled with triangular slices of watermelon. THANK YOU, LORD! The watermelon was not only refreshing, but it quenched my parched throat like it was never dry. I had three slices, and when I finished guzzling them down, I felt like brand new. Okay, now I'm ready for the second part of the hike of the vertical climb up. I was feeling more energetic now, but I was still exhausted. What a hike that was. When I came near to the end of this mountain there was another plateau and…. oh, my goodness it was over. I could see our campsite in the very near distance and all the vehicles. I did it…we did it!

In His Presence

Every day is the day we walk in the presence of our Father.

Every day we experience the joy which the day brings.

Every day we are happy and optimistic.

Every day we exist we share our love to the world.

Take each day at a time, and the peace that surpasses all understanding shall be yours.

Every day is the day I walk in the present with my Father.

Every day I watch my dreams unfold before my eyes.

Every day I experience the joy which the day brings.

Every day I wake up happy and optimistic.

Every day I exist I share my love with the world.

Knowing that every day the peace that surpasses all understanding is mine.

Anna Elena Gordon

1st Thought – Ego and Emotions

I am at the point in my life where I think that I am grasping at straws. I don't have a significant other, and sometimes I wish I had one, but something is going on where either I meet someone, and they don't care about communicating and wait for me to call ALL the time or I meet someone where they only appear to be interested in the physical aspect of a relationship. Or, I meet someone who appears to be interested and caring and then they do the complete opposite and show their other side when I open my heart to them.

I must say that I have met some very interesting male acquaintances that just don't cut it. After all these years something is desperately wrong. But wrong with who? Is it me? Or is it him? Am I too critical or is he just not interested in what I'm interested in and I realize that we are not compatible?

Of course, the ever-ready ego says it's him, and then emotionally I get all distraught thinking that men can't handle my candidness and my straightforwardness and telling the truth is a killer of romances. So be gone with them! But then the emotions kick in, and they tell me I made a mistake and that I came on too strong or maybe I should at least try and be a tiny bit submissive…but sorry, that's not my make-up.

My children tell me that I'm T.M.I. – Give too much information. Again, I'm an open book and speak on whatever comes to my mind…ok, ok then you are dealing with: Anna (id); Elena (ego) and Aneska (superego) and believe it or not, I don't know which one has more control. I rather think that Anna does, but then sometimes Elena slips out of nowhere living in the past messing things up allowing constant noise and then out pops Aneska trying to figure things out by assuming things which gets Anna in some serious trouble because the assumptions are always wrong.

So…I'm alone. Not lonely now just alone. I don't mind being by myself. Matter of fact, I have learned to embrace my being alone with fantasies, creativity, books, movies, music, singing, dancing and traveling…blogging of course. But, the bottom line is my expression of freedom is intimidating to men. So…where do I go from here?

Is someone supposed to find me and love me at first sight? Have they done that already and when I open my mouth they change their mind? What a terrible thought, ugh!

I'm just not getting it. Maybe this time in my life I'm not supposed to be with anyone. Sure, there are many out there that I could throw myself on and trust me they would catch me, but I don't want a fling.

I want to be happy with dating one guy or…maybe two. They don't need to know each other, but they need to be promising and single, to make things interesting.

Anna Elena Gordon

The Spirit

Every life is a book of secrets, ready to be opened by unlocking the hidden dimensions of your life each day at a time. Each secret will bring you closer to your true core and find your divine purpose, only if you dare to reveal yourself to YOU.

Exposure

It was a beautiful Sunday morning. The date was July 2010. I had decided to wear my maxi olive linen dress with my big white wide brim hat. The morning was quiet, and I was anticipating a wonderful service in the Lord's house. As I entered the church building, people started arriving as well, and the praise team was preparing to start ministering in song. As I sat down, which was usually behind the pastor's seat in the second row, I felt my spirit becoming uneasy. I started feeling like something was about to happen. I had felt this feeling a few times before. The feeling where The Holy Spirit which is The Comforter to some was nudging me. I heard that soft-spoken voice that only I can hear, telling me to expose myself…expose me.

Now, I have a best friend who never shares my secrets, my pain, my hurts, my heart bruises. He keeps my secrets, and He is the only one I had told this adultery situation too. I would reason with him, justifying my actions. I would at one point convince myself that I needed to stop doing these things and for a while, I would stop. But my friend knew that I hadn't made up my mind to stop. So, when I finally got tired of being like this which was beginning to cause problems in my life and the lives of others, I couldn't take it any longer. I started praying wholeheartedly, this time, asking God to please take this demon away. Now you must also understand that my best friend is God. He is the only one who I told this to, and He knew right then when I prayed this time that I was sincere. I was tired of this life. God always answers my prayers when I give 100% to Him when I have an issue that needs resolved. I never know when the answer will come, but I do know that my faith has always been strong enough to believe that whatever I pray for I will receive. I don't waiver nor do I doubt! I call this my "crazy faith" which is what I believe I have in God. So, on this particular Sunday, I got my answer. Unfortunately for me, it wasn't quite the answer that I thought I would get.

"I want you to expose yourself" is what I kept hearing deep within me. Man, I knew what my spirit was talking about too. I started sweating; my legs started shaking, and I didn't want to do it. I couldn't see myself telling this congregation…anybody for that matter my secret! It was between God and me. No way! BUT, I know me, too. I know when these feelings come on me, no matter what the subject matter, no matter who it is for, I must be obedient and speak what God tells me to speak.

As the praise team started to sing, my pastor was entering the room and saw my face. It was a face she hadn't seen before, so immediately she asked me what was wrong. I told her that I had to speak on something and she asked me what. I told her that God wanted me to expose myself to my secret. She looked at me again and said that I needed to say it. So, now what? I had no idea how I was going to do this. I asked the Lord, I said, "Father if you want me to do this you are going to have to show me how." I will never forget those words. Shortly after, and I mean quickly, I was led to Psalms 51, the penitent's psalm and at that very moment, my pastor told the congregation that I had something to share. I had to give testimony, and I heard my spirit say that it wasn't about me. Anna this is not about you. I stood in front of the congregation reading the Psalm. I was fine until I got to about the 6th verse when the tears just started streaming down my face. My vision became so blurry that I could hardly see the rest of the Psalm. I stopped at verse 17, I do believe, and then I was able to testify about my addiction as an adulterer and how I was also smoking cannabis. When I finished, I felt whole and complete! I started weeping but also praising God! I saw some of the church members standing and giving praises to God. A few moments into my praising, I fell on my knees bowing to My Holy of Holies and giving Him glory. Women, one by one, were coming around me telling me thank you and how they too were going through the same thing but didn't know how to speak on it. I was amazed by their confessions secretly whispering them in my ear which was low to the ground.

It wasn't about me at all. God had again used me to bless someone with my testimony and give them hope that God can heal anyone from anything when you give Him all. It was a beautiful service after that. A wonderful sweet spirit permeated in that place, and that is a day that I will never forget.

Oh, by the way, that lustful demon never bothered me again. He was exposed. Since that Sunday in July 2010, I have not witnessed that lustful demon again. It is now 2015! Glory to God!!!

What I am about to reveal took all my strength and courage to expose hoping that this experience will heal someone and not judge for the choices we make.

Deception

I am angry at myself first for not wanting my children. I can't seem to blame the men that I was fornicating with because I didn't want to have another baby by either of them who I thought I loved. There wasn't any future that I could see at the time where I would have wanted them to remain in my life. To make them care for an unwanted child seemed cruel to me. I didn't want anyone to know my business and for me to get pregnant by them and to carry their child for nine months would make me feel more ashamed than the act itself.

I was hurt and didn't want any more obligations to deal with by myself. I felt that these unsanctioned relationships were built on my desires and strength alone and I didn't want to hear anything - so I aborted.

God, you know what I have gone through with these men. You did not give consent to my fornication. I know that I was being disobedient when I did it, but because of my lustful and promiscuous manner, I did it anyway.

My mind was talking to me convicting me of this shamefulness I inflicted on myself instead of listening to my heart. WOW, I would have had eight children, Lord. Eight beautiful children-the Brady Bunch for real. I can't even imagine that. I would have had children from four different men? My 16-year-old boyfriend and his mother wanted my first born. I thought I did too until everybody kept on harping on education. All they thought about was our education. How young we were and look at the mess we got ourselves into at 15 and 16 years old. All that mattered was their pride! If I had strong individuals to tell me there was NO option, I would have carried my first baby full term. They told me aborting at 3 ½ months was still okay. It didn't matter, and I had until the fetus was five months. That was when he/she started forming. And I believed them! They told me not to tell anyone; it was a private matter. I couldn't see my boyfriend again-no communication. I was told to stay away from him. Their ungodly pride caused me to kill my child. They told me to continue and go to college; meet a doctor or lawyer and raise a family.

WAIT…STOP!!!

I feel like running!

I'm getting upset. My ears are getting clogged!

I'm getting hot and feeling depressed and flustered!

I'm feeling so very alone. I'm feeling some emotions surfacing that I thought were gone-hidden-leaving me alone for eternity…

But they are back…back. Back!

I don't like the way I am feeling right now. I must stop thinking about this for a moment. Got to do something else Lord. I will write another time.

Hello Father,

Here I am again wanting to continue with my purging. I'm feeling better today. I'm still having a time remembering the details.

Psalms 139:23-24 "Search me thoroughly, O God and know my heart, try me and know my thoughts and see if there is any wicked or hurtful way in me, and lead me in the way everlasting."

Why did I think that aborting was the right thing to do? They told me that if I loved them…hmmm! But as you well know, Father, the fourth one impregnated someone else telling me that I was the only one… and she had his BABY! Why didn't I do that? Why did I fall for the oki doki? Was that real love?

Good Morning Father,

Today is a great day. All days are wonderful when I listen to "How Great is Our God." Truly, Father, you are GREAT! I'm thanking you once again for your glory and wondrous works you have done for me. Truly You are Great! Just taking this time to give you glory and honor for all you have done in my life. How you are waking up a sleeping giant that has manifested and festered in my soul. It is time for me to face that impious giant for who it is so that I can send it on in love. It has suppressed and silenced the wound of abortion hurts long enough. It is time to stand up to this malignant spirit and face it face to face without malice; without strife; without bitterness; without anger and fear. These emotions have been because of this giant wound. This giant wound that has been storing and embracing fugitives, harboring them to the point where they went deep in my subconsciousness with no ambition of surfacing to hear what I now have to say. Today, they must hear me say, "thank you for protecting me from my subliminal pain, and I appreciate the fact that you kept me from hurting myself by blocking out all of the abortions that I have had. Not remembering caused me to move forward without realizing and experiencing a lot of symptoms of bitterness, but now that I understand that your job is complete, I expose you to move on. I awaken you to detach yourself from my core commanding the very selective and manipulative fugitive to uproot itself from my inner being. Now understanding and being enlightened, you will be removed immediately and be no more in my life. Go now in love and disentangle from my mind, body, and soul. In the Name of Jesus, you have been set free and so have I. Your time in my life has ended. I rebuke you!"

Father God, I am plucking this sore from my core from the root of all suffering asking you to forgive me for harboring this fugitive for so very long. Thanking you for allowing me to see that I needed to

Anna Elena Gordon

forgive myself even more so than forgiving all the participants that influenced me to abort.

Father God, I know this letter is lengthy and has gone on for a couple of days, but it has taken me time to digest and surface my mental wounds that have been hiding and sheltering in my core my soul my essence.

Thank you, Comforter,
Thank you, Holy Spirit
Thank you, Jesus
Thank you, God, from whom all blessings flow.
In Jesus Name

To My Unborn Babies,

Thank you for forgiving me. Forgive me for not knowing or understanding or caring. These emotions caused me to abort. My beautiful children! I don't even know your genders. I guess that when I got off the metal table I didn't ask, and they didn't say although I do know that one of you is a boy. I wish we could have spent more time together. You would have loved your other siblings. They are precious. Two of them would be with you now had I not the courage to speak up. Because, of you, I now can say, "no" during those times. I know you have forgiven me because I feel FREE. I know that you are sitting with our Father in heaven as his angels of protection, safety, healing, deliverance, and soundness, the Solteria, and I will always love you as much as my children of the flesh. I am so sorry that I took your physical attributes your presence away from me and the world. Only God has given me this enlightenment and unspeakable joy that I have at this time. I am so proud and honored to be your mother. You four munchkins will always have a deep place in my heart and love that goes beyond what man can comprehend or fathom.

Love you,
Momsy

Anna Elena Gordon

During the following week, I was discussing guilt and shame with my spiritual guide. I began to reminisce about periodical times when I was raising my children. Times when I experienced hurt-emotional stress-anxiety-depression.

Suddenly, guilt started rolling up my back from my core like a heavy surge of heat and pressure. My back felt like someone was pushing down on me with a metal plate. My head started getting warm causing my face to fluster. My vision became luminous, but everything appeared to be dark but vivid. (Hard to describe this unwanted surge of emotions.) My body felt like someone was hovering over me like the inside of a balloon with all the pressure about to burst. That as guilt! This last bit of guilt-creeping up on my neck from my essence trying to attack my body and mind...ohhh, it had to go! My occiput was beginning to get tight. Suddenly, I was feeling drained. Guilt I thought was gone. Guilt I thought had released when I exposed things in anger and forgiveness. Guilt-all of it had not let go because of what I was experiencing. My spiritual guide started praying in her heavenly language. She prayed until God told her to stop. After she prayed, I only felt the guilt on the right side of my body and head. Then we started reading the Word of God. We then continued our mission exposing guilt and shame through the Word. Our lesson continued.

A few days later, I felt that guilt had left me alone. I started rejoicing and praising God because that is how guilt and shame began to be released. Through prayer and praise, I had surrendered and gave guilt and shame to God.

Good Day Father,

Today is the first day where it is just you and me. I'm taking time out for me. Starting today with fasting and praying. Hearing the birds chirp, looking at the bright sunshine blindly on the snow at 25 degrees-what a beautiful day.

My spiritual guide and I finished the program, loving every class – purging all remembrances of the sin and eradicating my inner being to have peace and joy in the innermost parts of my mind. God, this purging, this cleaning, this opening up the scars to see what was inside was purifying. The abortion was keloid over with lots and lots of wounded fibrous tissue wanting to be touched once again by the hand of God which was now mending the time frozen wound. My scar was deep under the hardened mass to the point of non-existence. It had become reprobated and lost to my mind. But your plan God was to pluck it from the distorted keloid and expose it to the world, so I can now breathe again! The fugitive inside my inner being had to repent; to forgive; to love. I thank you, God, for allowing me to go through the hurt-the guilt-the shame-the pain that has been plaguing my thought process. The purging is what I needed finally exposing the reason why I acted certain ways. I am free once again to live a holy and loved life. This abortion thing was a crucial turning point in my life. During this transition, I have gained new revelation, and it has taken my faith to another level.

I AM FREE!

Anna Elena Gordon

Deception

If indeed my womb is carrying nothing

Then how can nothing have a gender

If indeed what was planted is not growing

Then how can the planted have a gender

If indeed when you get off that cold table after being vacuumed out

Why would they ask you, "do you want to know the gender?"

If indeed life starts then stops with you

Then you and they already know there is a gender

Life begins with a seed. All of God's creation begins with a seed.

The flowers that bloom, the fish in the sea, the birds in the air, the walking and crawling animals and the insects.

All the creeping things upon the earth begins with a seed.

When man and woman join together man implants a seed that touches woman's unfertilized egg making it become life. Fertility begins with a seed

Life is that seed. That is how it begins.

Yes, abortion is killing!

Yes, abortion is killing!

Yes, abortion is killing a beautiful seed that is destined to be great before God.

NO MORE KILLING

Allow that seed to grow and miraculously become an arm, a leg, a head, a torso with fingers and toes and with a beautiful mind.

Don't be deceived

Deception is a killer!

It Was Me!

Today is a day with a new attitude. For the last three days, I have been praising God so passionately. Three days ago, I called upon a seasoned woman, a woman of God that prays all the time. She blessed me with scriptures and words of wisdom that have been blessing me ever since. All God wants us to do is praise him. I think that now I can truly begin to understand if we praise God and watch him bless, everyone would have more than enough. Everyone would then believe and become highly favored. When the praises to the Lord go up, the blessings of the Lord come down. I love to praise him. I'm beginning to appreciate praise more and more. Peace comes with praises; joy comes with praises; revelations come with praises; excitement comes with praises. I want to read more about prayer-interceding for others. I am reading a book entitled, "Intercessory Prayer" by Dutch Sheets.

I'm looking forward to receiving a blessing from this book and an encouraged heart.

Jack Hayford said, "prayer is essentially a partnership of the redeemed child of God working hand in hand with God toward the realization of his redemptive purposes on earth."

I just realized that that ugly, deceptive, non-loving, unkind, dirty and cunning controlling spirit was coming from ME! Oh, my GOD!

This spirit is the residue of my abortion symptoms and plagues which captured my very essence since the age of 15. Oh Lord, how wonderful and how crafty is your love towards me. You have once again opened my eyes and ears to more revelation.

He Knows What He is Doing

GOD KNOWS WHAT HE IS DOING WHEN YOUR EYES OPEN IN THE MORNING, AND YOU CAN SEE

GOD KNOWS WHAT HE IS DOING WHEN THE FIRST THING YOU UTTER FROM YOUR MIND TO LIPS IS AN ACKNOWLEDGEMENT OF HOW GREAT HE IS

GOD KNOWS WHAT HE IS DOING WHEN ALL HE ASKS US TO DO IS PRAISE HIM

GOD KNOWS WHAT HE IS DOING WHEN HE ORDERS OUR STEPS EVERY SECOND OF THE DAY

GOD KNOWS WHAT HE IS DOING WHEN YOUR SEED YOUR ESSENCE IS GUIDED BY HIS SPIRIT

GOD KNOWS HOW MUCH YOU CAN BEAR

GOD KNOWS THAT HE WILL ALWAYS MAKE A WAY FOR YOU TO ESCAPE

GOD KNOWS EVERYTHING

GOD SEES EVERYTHING

GOD HEARS EVERYTHING

OUR OMNISCIENT, OMNIPRESENT GOD; OUR SOVEREIGN, ALMIGHTY, EVERLASTING, ALL POWERFUL, MAGNIFICENT ABBA KNOWS WHAT HE IS DOING!

Peace...and Then There Is Peace

I thought I heard Him

I thought I heard my Father authenticating what I did not want

I thought I heard Him telling me to keep it a secret

I thought I was listening attentively...

I was fine by myself

I was enjoying life with my son, whom God had blessed me with one more time

I was now living a life of abstinence honoring my body after a world wind of promiscuity

I was now releasing the fugitives I was harboring since I was 15 years of age.

I thought I heard Him

I thought I heard Him

I went on a fast for three days denying all, waiting for an answer

Waiting for the answer to tell me it wasn't okay. That it wasn't God's will for me to alter my life

Because I was fine by myself

I was enjoying life with my son, whom God had blessed me with one more time

After praying, after seeking, after meditating, after giving all to whom I worship and praise daily

I received such peace

This peace came when I was struggling

This peace came when confusion had set in

This peace came as an answer to my question.

This peace came as a sign to go forward

But I was fine by myself…really?

Other than enjoying my life with my son could there be more?

Was I leaning on my understanding or was I acknowledging Him in all his ways?

Peace was my answer

Peace was my assurance that all was well

Peace gave me that joy and the confidence that my family would love my decision…so I thought

Peace….and then there is peace

This peace I received was temporary because after two months the peace was gone

After two months of accepting my altered lifestyle, the peace was diminishing

After two months of accepting my peace life was becoming chaotic

This peace is not the peace I know

This joy is not the joy I know

This life is not the lifestyle that I fasted to receive!

There is peace, and then there is peace

I want the peace that surpasses all understanding

I want the peace that brings God's agape love

I want the peace that gives me the confidence that all is well with my soul

I want the peace that the world can't give me; the peace that takes away sorrow, worry, confusion and fear

Wow…my peace was temporary

My peace was coming from my flesh

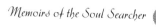

My peace was not given to me by my Father

Because, I am where I am now; because I did not confirm my peace; because I assumed; because I thought what I didn't want I should get...because of peace.

I was fine by myself

I was enjoying life with my son whom God had blessed me with for only one year...and now he is gone.

Peace...but then there is The Peace!

God's peace! BIG difference

I thought I hear Him

I thought I heard my Father authenticating what I did not want

I thought I heard Him telling me to keep it a secret

I thought I was listening attentively...

Anna Elena Gordon

Just Because

JUST BECAUSE I love you, does not mean that I like you

JUST BECAUSE I like you, does not mean that I want you

JUST BECAUSE I want you, does not mean that I need you

I love MY GOD

I like MY GOD

I want MY GOD

I need MY GOD

JUST BECAUSE you say you love me, does not mean that I understand you

JUST BECAUSE you say that you like me, does not mean that I trust you

JUST BECAUSE you say that you want me does not mean that I believe you

JUST BECAUSE you say you need me, does not mean that I have faith in you

I understand MY GOD

I trust MY GOD

I believe MY GOD

I have faith in MY GOD

JUST BECAUSE you say things, does not mean that you are speaking the truth

JUST BECAUSE you do things, does not mean that it is coming from your heart

MY GOD says that He will supply all my need according to his riches in glory

MY GOD says that He will never leave me or forsake me

MY GOD loves me so much that He gave his only begotten son

MY GOD wants me to dwell in His secret place

MY GOD wants me to understand that He is the lifter of my head

MY GOD loves me and has called me by my name…I am His

MY GOD is all these things to me

MY GOD does all these things for me

MY GOD says all these things to me

JUST BECAUSE!

Anna Elena Gordon

I choose unconditional love and understanding and trust and faith in someone. I choose the agape love that MY GOD has put inside every one of us. Dig deep and find it. Dig deep and bring it up and start applying it to your daily talk and walk.

Love on someone today

Hug on someone today

Give to someone today

Bless someone today

JUST BECAUSE!

My Jehovah-My Shepherd

Psalms 23

Anna's Amplified Version

September 28, 2012

The Lord is my shepherd, my Jehovah Rohi who feeds, who guides and shields me.

I shall not lack because my Jehovah Jireh provides for me and I shall not want for anything.

He makes me lie down in fresh, tender green pastures where my Jehovah Rapha begins to heal my mind, body, and soul. My Jehovah Shalom who provides peace leads me besides the still and restful waters where I hear Him speak to me.

He refreshes and restores my life, my Jehovah Mekaddishkem who continually sanctifies me; my Jehovah Tsidkenu, my Lord of Righteousness leads me in the paths of uprightness and right standing with Him-not for my earning it, but for his names' sake, Adonai, My Great Lord!

Yes, though I walk through the deep and sunless valley of the shadow of death with my El Shaddai, I will fear or dread no evil, because

El Roi, my God who sees me, you are with me; Your rod to protect and Your staff to guide, they comfort me because of my Elohim, my All-Powerful One.

You, Jehovah Shammah, The Lord who is there, prepare a table of provisions to bear, to endure and outlast before me in the presence of my enemies. You, my Jehovah Elyon, my Lord Most High anoint my head with oil, my brimming cup runs over.

Surely and only goodness, mercy and unfailing love, THE GLORY shall follow me all the days of my life, and through the length of my days in the house of the Lord, my Jehovah Sabaoth, my Lord of Hosts and His presence shall be my dwelling place.

Reveal the You in Me

Father God, as I sit here pondering what to write and meditating on why I married two times, I am considering your ways. I am contemplating on how You always reveal yourself to me in such a mysterious manner. I never know how or when. I don't question You anymore on the whys…because You are El Shaddai and know all and whatever happened I am because you allowed it. So here I'm asking myself what this title, Reveal the You in Me is all about.

As I was sharing with my dear spiritual mother various reasons for my marriages, not yet fully understanding the men I married, she was telling me that God sometimes will allow people in your life for you to grow closer to Him. As she was speaking the revelation of the way I got married became so apparent.

Sometimes God, the manifestation of Your mercy and grace is being tested through our sincerity and integrity which makes our Christ-like nature truly transparent. We who are the chosen ones are being watched, tried and tested every second, minute and hour of the day; undoubtedly by our adversary, but also by our omniscient Father who watches and sees our faith in Him. For without faith it is impossible to please Him. It is impossible even to get close to Him if you don't believe in Him because He is only a rewarder to them that diligently are seeking him.

In other words, because I have been seeking the answer to these riddled marriages of mine you, Father, revealed to me the reason for my marriages. I finally realize that my marriages were bruised and broken-hearted individuals seeking love. Both of us KNOWING the truth but wanting a wife and husband to stand by us understanding where we were, carnally and spiritually. Yes, I was that wife, and these broken individuals were placed in my life because I believe God, you allowed this type of behavior. I called them from my subconsciousness which allowed these types of men to become a reality in my life.

Would I alter my spiritual life with my Father because of this turmoil?! WOW!!! Are you kidding me? Let me quote something from the bestselling book of our time: The Bible, which reads in Romans 8:37-39, "Yet and all these things we are more than conquerors and gain a surpassing victory through Him who loved us. For I am persuaded beyond doubt, am sure, that neither death nor life, nor angels nor principalities, nor things impending and threatening nor things to come, nor powers, nor height nor depth, nor anything else in all creation will be able to separate us from the love of God which is in Christ Jesus our Lord." This quote is real to me. It has given me the backbone to persevere through tribulation, distress, persecution, hunger, and destitution. I know I am more than a conqueror. So, with such a backbone and then having to deal with these mates being as broken as we are and the love that I have for them, I cannot allow that to interfere with my walk with my Father. God, you allowed me to see drug addiction, double-mindedness, schizophrenic manipulative personalities in these persons who would then become as humble and sweet and loving. Talking about a journey; talking about walking through the valley of the shadow of death where I feared no evil for You God provided provisions and my assurance of who You are even in this.

All I can say now is that my soul is becoming more and more satisfied in the revelation that You are placing before me one season at a time because only You Lord know how much I can bear at once. You are magnificently revealing who I am in You and the more I seek and find the more I am loving the how, the when, the who and the why You are placing in my life.

So, Lord, I thank you, and I praise you and give you the glory at all times for what you are proving about yourself to me repeatedly, and I thank You for "Revealing the You in Me." Amen

It is me that causes things to happen

It is me that chooses right from wrong

What is right and what is wrong?

Everyone has hidden dimensions of who they are

Anyone can tap into the etheric energy to manifest thoughts that are valid enough to spring forth

A thought materializes when we dwell on it. When it sparks, we catch it, and it becomes.

Our thoughts are what gets us what we want and don't want

It is nothing but pure energy floating around the universal sphere waiting, anticipating one live being catching some of what it has to offer. Some catch a lot, and some catch not so much

We are life...we are part of this miraculous and phenomenal field gathered into a humongous circle called planet being able to obtain anything we want!

Do you believe that?

Do you even comprehend that?

Would you dare think like this?

Would you please come out of your attached self: attached to this and that; attached to business that is not yours and detach your brain to engulf the miraculous...visualize the phenomena;

I dare you

I implore you

You will become, you will start to see, you will start to dream; you will start to meditate and pull into yourself all that you desire which is nothing but bliss: kindness, creativity, abundance, explorations, receiving all, and love.

We would be celebrating in a place within us where we are both on one accord living life in the present where the moment is now. A free spirit soaring like an eagle through life in the now.

We are life…we can do whatever we please, desire and want. We can manifest whatever we please, desire and want.

We are human life…we have dominion over all other life. We are in control of all.

So, I ask you:

Why is there poverty? Why is there chaos? Why is there killing? Why is there war?

Those humans that initiate this type of behavior causes an imbalance in their world which creeps into the inner pockets of our planet seeping into the weak minded.

I chose to believe that the world and everyone in it have something good for me. I also chose to believe that the world and everyone in it protects me and provides for me because of the unconditional love that I spread every waking moment of the day. Unconditional love flows through me attracting and creating wonderful relationships.

Stay in the now where there is peace and love. Don't manifest thoughts that you allow to take you back to the past. Stay in the present and secure your thoughts from the ego.

Namaste

Anna Elena Gordon

Is That It?

Is that the crazy faith I have been talking about practically all my life?

Was having crazy faith an indication of how I was feeling about myself?

Was my saying, "I have crazy faith," talking about why I am the way I am?"

In other words

I have crazy faith because I know that I have the faith in me to believe in me.

My crazy faith is in me.

If I can manifest anything I want by a mere thought: we all can manifest thoughts.

"...as man thinketh so is he." (Bible verse) Our thoughts become verbalized which becomes atmospheric which then grabs hold of a universal spark which then miraculously locates other thoughts of common gratitude which then get together and manifest our verbalized thoughts into existence.

Is that it?

If this is the crazy I have been experiencing all my life which I recall began at the age of 5, then indeed that universal energy is mine, and it is for the taking. We are human, superhuman, supernatural energy beings enveloped by our Source which is Universal Energy which is Spirit.

The Source is the omniscient, omnipotent, omnipresent Source, which has many names all over the world like God, Abba, The Holy One, Jehovah, King of Kings, The Creator, etc. which I know exist. I am part of The Source, an heir. Therefore I, we can have whatsoever we please.

That crazy faith is mine.

Therefore, whatever I ask for I receive.

There is nothing I want that I don't obtain.

My thoughts verbalize into the atmosphere, and a universal shifting begins to manifest into existence.

That is it!

"Our deepest fear is not that we are inadequate; our deepest fear is that we are powerful beyond measure. It is our light, not our darkness, that frightens us. We ask ourselves, "Who am I to be brilliant, gorgeous, talented and fabulous?" Actually, who are you not to be? You are a child of God. Your playing small doesn't serve the world. There's nothing enlightened about shrinking so other people won't feel insecure around you. We were born to manifest the glory of God within us.

It's not just in some of us; it's in everyone. And as we let our light shine, we unconsciously permit other people to do the same. As we are liberated from our own fear, our presence automatically liberates others."

Nelson Mandella, 1994 Inaugural Speech

Printed in the United States
By Bookmasters